A GIFT FOR
FROM

Editorial Director: Todd Hafer

Editors: Jeff Morgan & Trieste Van Wyngarden

Art Director: Kevin Swanson

Designer: Michelle Nicolier

Production Art: Dan Horton

Printed and bound in China.

ISBN: 1-59530-128-3

First Edition, March 2006

10 9 8 7 6 5 4 3 2 1

BOK4310

Teachers
touch lives

GIFT BOOKS
from Hallmark

IN MEMORY OF

Thomas Meidell Johnson

dedicated teacher,

admirable person.

INTRODUCTION

Teachers are everyday heroes. They inspire hopes, nurture dreams, and encourage success. They seek out potential and find ways to develop it. They coach the talented, comfort the troubled, reward achievement, and promote good character. Teachers step in front of their rows of students each day and offer the world. The stories collected here are a testament to the lasting impressions teachers make. Their actions and personalities are remembered with gratitude and appreciation years, even decades, after a student moves on—proving that what teachers share are truly lessons for a lifetime.

A good teacher
is the perfect
balance of firmness
and understanding,
of guidance
and freedom,
OF MENTOR
AND FRIEND.

JUST LIKE FAMILY

The first day at a new school can be terrifying. Just ask my orchestra teacher, Miss Reece. We started junior high school on the same day. I, at least, had the benefit of a few carryover friends from sixth grade. For Miss Reece, all the faces were new. As she stuttered and blushed her way through that first practice, I felt an immediate kinship with her. Not only did she love music, but just like me, she was nervous, unsettled by this new place.

Although she eventually became more self-assured in the classroom, Miss Reece never developed that defensive attitude that seemed a natural reaction to teen sarcasm and homework excuses. On stage, when she held her baton up to begin, her eyes would plead for our very best effort, and we would know how important our performance was to her. In class, when she would ask about a student's well-being, she would wait for the answer with genuine concern. And when a violist asked whether Miss Reece had gotten a new ring, she gushed that she had been engaged for nearly three days and was wondering when we would finally notice!

Nervous, hopeful, concerned, or excited, Miss Reece shared so much more with her students than her knowledge of strings and music. She shared herself, and that made us all feel like family.

Jill Reed

She shared
so much

GO AS FAR AS YOU CAN

Fourth grade was my favorite year of elementary school. The classroom was packed; our school had recently absorbed two other small school districts from neighboring communities. But Miss Southard had been teaching since my mother was a pupil in the one-room-schoolhouse days, and she maintained order with both dignity and humor.

Early in the school year, she placed the more advanced students at a rear table and handed out dog-eared eighth-grade math books and a teacher's manual with the answers in the back. "Go as far as you can," she instructed and returned to the front of the classroom. Periodically, she checked and cheered our progress, meanwhile devoting most

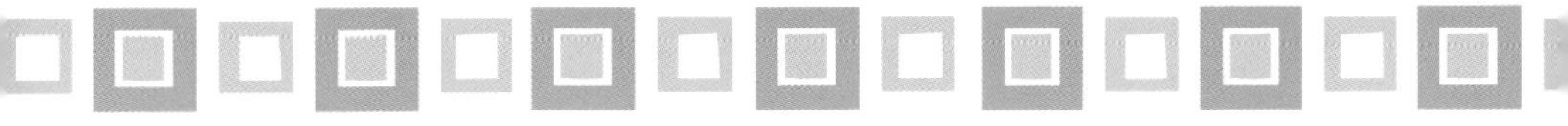

of her energies to those struggling to master fourth-grade math. As we learned to do square roots and find the value of *x* and *y*, we also learned valuable lessons in leadership, group dynamics, ethics, and teamwork. By year's end, we had finished the book.

Miss Southard understood the power of praise and the motivation of a challenge. "Go as far as you can," she'd said; and we did. If some of us are still going, still growing, still having fun learning, it's because Miss Southard and others like her taught us, encouraged us, believed in us, inspired us—a tradition that continues today in classrooms everywhere.

Keely Chace

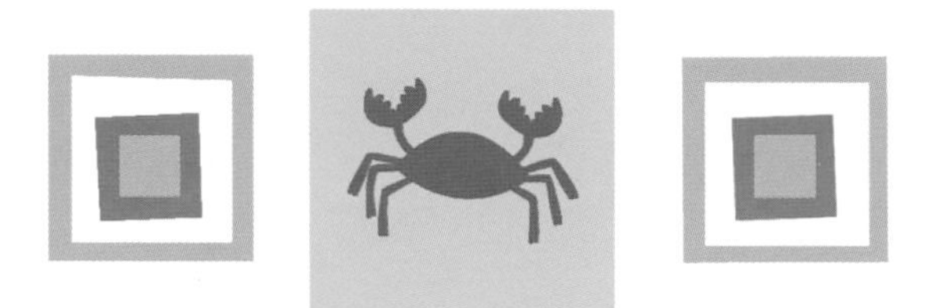

A NOVEL APPROACH

At first I wasn't Mrs. Terrell's most-prized second-grade student. Maybe it all started when I brought a crab shell from the Shoney's dinner menu for show-and-tell or the day I got caught playing kissing games at recess. Maybe it was because I was the only girl with a mullet. Whatever it was, I was terrified of Mrs. Terrell.

But one thing I loved about her class was creative writing. We wrote stories and poetry and journal entries. We even got to write to the local newspaper editor. I wrote a politically incorrect letter about, of all things, politics and suddenly learned the magic of editing.

One day, we had to write about the different types of clouds. I wrote a poem about cumulus clouds. Later that week, just as school was letting out, Mrs. Terrell stopped my mother in the hallway and handed her my poem. This cannot be good, I thought.

"She's going to write a novel someday," my teacher said in her tough, no-nonsense way. I froze. Could this be a compliment? From Mrs. Terrell?

It was. And after that day, second grade turned out to be not so bad. Also, more than ever before, I dreamed of being a writer when I grew up.

Thanks, Mrs. Terrell, for believing in me. Today, for show-and-tell, I brought... my writing.

Katherine Stano

I still think of him

LIVING HISTORY

Mr. Smith was my ninth-grade history teacher, but he didn't just teach history, he lived it.

He would act out each new topic, complete with costumes, and give a full dramatic recounting of a speech, battle, or declaration.

He knew if he merely recited dates and names, the important real-life experiences might be lost on us. We'd run to his class to see the show (and because if we arrived mid-performance, we'd be pulled on stage to become a Roman soldier or a minuteman).

I was a decent student, but my history grades were always a bit better than "decent." When I took his exams, I wouldn't be straining to remember facts but actually reliving the event in my head. Sometimes, Mr. Smith would even wear the costume from that lesson on exam day!

Later in high school, I would see Mr. Smith walking the halls, wearing his Roman soldier's helmet or George Washington wig. And sometimes up in math class or over in English, I'd hear him yelling, "Friends, Romans, countrymen!" or "We the people!"

I had a chance to thank him recently for his talent and energy. I told him that when I see period costumes on TV, I still think of him on stage, reminding me why a certain moment in history was so important.

Chris Conti

DEMANDING OUR BEST

Mrs. Reynolds was a force to be reckoned with. If you got her for seventh-grade English, you either feared her, adored her or, in my case, both.

Imagine a loud, formidable woman with a powerful stride and huge silver hairdo, wafting a mixture of teacher's-lounge coffee and heavy-duty Tigress perfume—amazing! She took no crap; that much was clear. But, oh, how she loved us when we were good...and gave us opportunities to shine. We wrote and illustrated our very own "Myths," spending a week working on our hands and knees with markers and long rolls of butcher paper, making murals. We even diagrammed sentences with the heart-pounding desire to make her smile.

Even those boys who played the school tough guys fell under her spell and often won her favor. Mrs. Reynolds would have made a top-notch drill sergeant. But I'm glad she chose to serve her country in the classroom instead. Every kid who came out of there came out a little taller, carrying a special something inside–something that would shape his or her destiny for years to come.

Respect. She demanded our best and awarded us the ultimate honor, her respect. That we also learned English, well, that was merely a bonus.

Jeannie Hund

GOOD ADVICE

It was my junior year at the university and time to choose classes for the new semester. I'd penciled in a schedule for myself as always, beginning with my required classes, then adding a few easy classes to lighten my load and make time for socializing. I felt certain that this year's randomly assigned advisor would scan the enrollment card, sign it, and hand it back, just as the others had.

But I was wrong. "No, no, no," she said, looking at my records and my plan for the semester. "I see students like you all the time, taking easy classes, missing opportunities to challenge yourself." She picked up a pen. "I'm signing you up for Shakespeare," she said, writing over my pencil marks, "and Communications Law." I tried to explain that I had a part-time job, that these classes were too difficult, that I didn't want to mess up my grade point average, but she ignored me. "Stop wasting your time and potential," she said simply. She signed the enrollment card. My fate was sealed.

I learned a lot about Shakespeare and communications law that semester, but I learned something else, too: That I was capable of more. That somebody cared enough to pick me up off one track and set me on another, better one... that it was a gift to have an advisor like her, even if just for a few minutes.

Jennifer Fujita

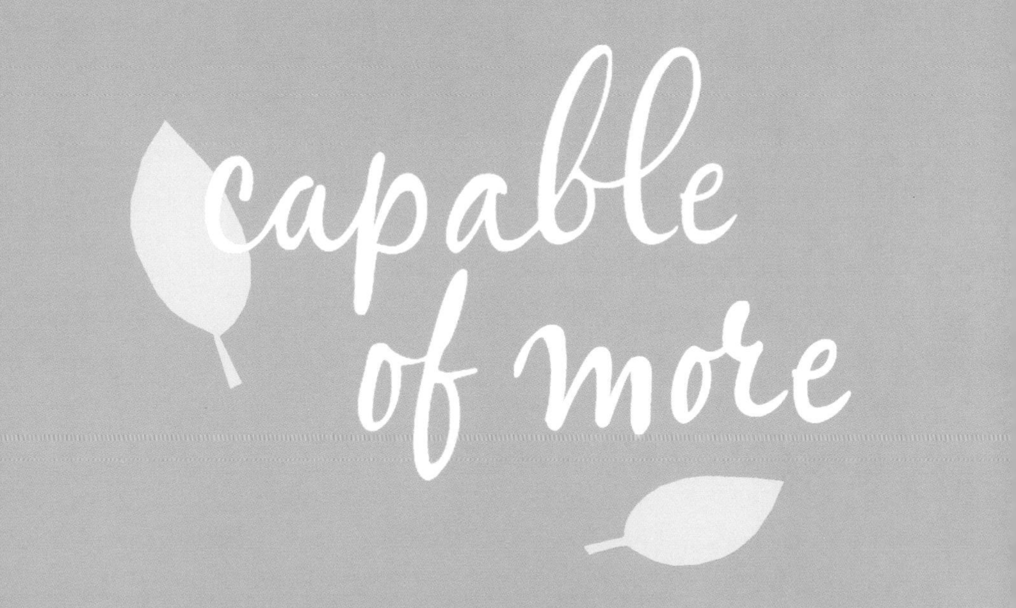
capable
of more

MAKING SHAKESPEARE COOL

When I started tenth grade, I finally got to pick the English class I wanted to attend. Up until that time, students attended a required, basic English class for their grade. I no longer can remember why I chose the Shakespeare class, but quite possibly I chose it because of the teacher, Mrs. Clouse. I had seen her many times in the crowded hallways, and she looked really cool. She had short, spiky hair and the coolest shoes.

Plus, she had a poster of Bruce Springsteen in her classroom for no other reason than she thought he was sexy.

The best thing about Mrs. Clouse, though, had to be how enthusiastically she taught Shakespeare. It was contagious. I would read the assigned portion of the play at home, and when I came to class the next day, it sprang to life as Mrs. Clouse helped us figure out what it all meant. She gave Shakespeare a current, hip feel. The ability of anything to capture my imagination and interest at 15 other than boys was pretty amazing.

We were allowed to joke around a little and be ourselves completely in her classroom. She was a teacher who seemed to take true joy in teaching, and that made it a joy to be in her class.

Allyson Jones

The smallest
gifts of caring
and attention
make the
BIGGEST
DIFFERENCE.

OKAY TO CRY

What I remember most about fourth grade isn't the times tables, the snow days, or the state capitols. What I remember so vividly are the times when Mrs. Sears cried. She cried often. Every year without fail, Mrs. Sears cried when we sang "Silent Night" at the Christmas program. She cried when she read us the life story of Martin Luther King, Jr. She cried when Leslie fell on the playground and had to get stitches. She cried while handing out hugs on the last day of school. She cried when we tied yellow ribbons on the flagpole for the soldiers.

At a time in my life when I was supposed to be a "big kid" and never shed a tear, it was such a lesson in empathy to see this kindhearted woman whom I admired so much show such compassionate emotion. She taught me that it was okay to share my feelings. She cried when I sobbed to her that my parents were divorcing.

Some may call her unprofessional. But we all just knew her as the beloved teacher who would always hold your hand and would never tell you "don't cry." And who always had plenty of tissues.

Amy Trowbridge

I admired her so much

LAUGHING IN SPANISH

Some teachers influence their students in ways they might never suspect. Miss Cummings did when she taught me Spanish in high school more years ago than I care to admit.

Her former students all said she was tough. Anyone who reached her classroom had already studied one year of Spanish, so she insisted on her standards. We were not to speak one word of English. Stammering and hesitant, we searched our memories for the words we needed. But newfound skills stayed with us because we used them constantly. And she had a sense of humor. Returning to the room once after a brief absence and finding us giggling, she shook her finger and teased, "Ah-ah-ah! Laugh in Spanish!"

She inspired us to love the melodious language that for some of us became even more important after graduation. I became a telephone operator, able to handle a switchboard where calls were made daily to Mexico. Even years later, in Oaxaca, I found myself translating for other travelers who spoke only English. What I learned as a teenager, thanks to Miss Cummings' dedication, has remained with me ever since. It has enriched my life and opened doors to friendships that otherwise I would never have made.

"*Muchísimas gracias, Señorita Cummings—¡Que Dios le bendiga a usted!*" (Many, many thanks, Miss Cummings—and may God bless you!)

Myra Zirkle

A BOOST FROM MRS. MASON

In fourth grade, I dreaded going to school every Tuesday. That was the day I had my weekly violin lesson after classes.

I liked violin. What I didn't like was the teasing and name-calling as I walked, violin case in hand, to and from my homeroom, where Mrs. Mason was my teacher. Being extremely shy, it wasn't long before I wanted to quit music lessons just to avoid the cruel jokes.

I can only guess that somehow Mrs. Mason found out what was happening, because one Tuesday, she asked me to play for the class. I was terrified... and secretly thrilled. Mrs. Mason was my favorite teacher, and I didn't want to disappoint her.

I played "Flow Gently, Sweet Afton" with my usual share of mistakes, but it didn't matter. Mrs. Mason began clapping, and the whole class joined in. She praised my effort and my courage in standing up in front of a crowd. After that, no one ever teased me about my violin again.

Looking back, I realize it wasn't so much my music that Mrs. Mason was interested in as my self-confidence, which she boosted tremendously that day.

I eventually gave up the violin. Don't even remember how to play anymore. But I'll never forget Mrs. Mason or her kindness on that special Tuesday many years ago.

Linda Staten

a daily period
of grace

STORY TIME

Mrs. Walters was a seasoned veteran—a no-nonsense teacher who could fold her arms across her chest and shut you down with just a look. She could deduct a point from your math test faster than you could say, "But..." And she was not above bringing in the school principal to bore the class with discipline tales from his Navy days.

You might not think a teacher like that would do story time, especially not for a bunch of unruly fourth graders who were getting too old for that sort of thing, anyway. But every day after recess, she pulled out a book and read to us, and for 20 minutes, we were perfect angels, totally engrossed in the story. Mrs. Walters' voice carried us to magical worlds and to real places, too. I especially remember a novel about a family heading west with a wagon train—pioneers, Indians, buffalo, all that good stuff. And I remember Mrs. Walters crying when one of the family members died. "Isn't this the saddest thing you've ever heard?" she asked us.

And it was sad. But it was also wonderful—to be read to, to be granted this little daily period of grace, and most of all, to see that our tough teacher was not only human but also a sucker for a good story. Just like us.

Keely Chace

LESS THAN PERFECT

My high school English teacher wasn't perfect, but he sure was fun. He made us read controversial books, then discuss social issues in class. He had a sharp wit and was quick to catch you in a Freudian slip. Sometimes he flirted with the girls or traded innuendoes with the boys. Naturally, we adored him.

I was a shy, bookish type, but his animated class discussions drew me out of my shell. He encouraged me to speak up, to be more of a leader, to take a few risks. He praised my poetry writing and helped me learn to craft sharp, clear essays. "You'll need this in college," he explained. "Um, yeah," I said.

College hadn't exactly been on my road map. I could easily get a secretarial job somewhere. College was expensive, and besides, school wasn't all that exciting.

But at his insistence, I took placement tests, filled out applications, wrote essays, and mailed transcripts. The rest is history—I graduated summa cum laude and wound up with a satisfying career as a writer.

Society today might call my teacher immature, even unprofessional. Certainly he was a kid who never grew up. But he was also a terrific teacher. And of all the things he taught us, perhaps this is the most important: you don't have to be perfect to make a difference.

Linda Barnes

take a
few risks

ACROSS TIME AND DISTANCE

On my first day of second grade in Peru, I was at a brand-new school. I didn't know anyone, and I was scared to death! But when I walked in, the teacher smiled at me and made me feel as if I were the most important person in the world. She was a missionary to my country and taught me with love, devotion, and a lot of fun thrown in. After that year in San José, my teacher went back to the States. I thought I would never see her again.

Fast-forward thirty-five years. One afternoon, to my amazement, I received a letter from that teacher asking me about my life and what had happened to me through the years! Immediately we began corresponding and were soon planning her return visit to Peru. When she came, the hug that she gave me told me just how deep a teacher's love can be. It touched me deeply to know that she had thought of me often, had prayed for me, and had longed to see me again. Now I proudly look back on the years gone by and look forward to new ones, knowing that there will always be one teacher who is very, very special to me.

Mary Miró

A GIFT FOR NURTURING

My daughter Sophie was heartbroken after our dog died unexpectedly. Even though she could barely stop crying, she didn't want to miss school the next day. I worried, but when I picked her up that afternoon, Sophie had a little smile on her face. She said that Mr. Ray, her homeroom teacher, had checked on her between classes, spent extra time talking with her, and gave Sophie little treats all through the day.

I already knew that Mr. Ray had a gift for nurturing a student's mind, but that day, he nurtured my daughter's heart as well. And in the process, I think he taught my daughter and the rest of his students something no textbook could offer—a quiet lesson in caring and compassion.

Linda Staten

A teacher takes a seed of **PROMISE**, tends it with encouragement, and watches as it grows...knowing that one day it will be the fruit that feeds the world.

A.K.A. THE RAZOR

We called Miss Gillette The Razor. There was her name, of course, but also her technique of slashing theme papers with red ink.

Every day in her high school English class, we studied the masters of English literature. And every night we wrote a paper.

One by one, we authors of red-inked sentences would bring Miss Gillette our rewrites, and one by one she'd rewrite them again. She was as kind as she was unyielding. Then it started to sink in. As in a car—where the crankshaft turns the driveshaft that turns the wheels—there are mechanics of good writing. If these aren't working, Miss Gillette taught us, your ideas don't go.

I began to pay more attention to the great writers and how they turned grammar and syntax into style, and style into genius. Through Miss Gillette, I met people who opened the world to me—Ernest Hemingway, Katherine Anne Porter, Flannery O'Connor, Emily Dickinson, Mark Twain, Willa Cather.

Who but a great friend would work so patiently, so thanklessly, to introduce me to people like that?

I didn't say it then, but I will now: Thank you, Miss Gillette—Teacher—wherever you are.

John Peterson

a great friend

A TIMELESS VIGOR

With her gray-streaked hair pulled back into a neat little bun and her signature black, high-button boots, Mrs. Smallwood looked as if she would have been more at home in a one-room schoolhouse in the 1880s than in my large, Midwestern high school in the 1980s. Yet there she was, every day, delivering English lessons in her own unique style.

Some people may have thought, based on her unconventional appearance, that she was outdated and out of touch, but those of us who knew her knew otherwise—we thought she was wonderful. Although she must have been nearing retirement age, Mrs.

Smallwood approached teaching with such youthful vigor that we just couldn't help but catch some of her excitement. She loved to read the classics. And read them, we did— *The Odyssey, Of Mice and Men, King Lear, Great Expectations*—they all came to life in Mrs. Smallwood's classroom, as her lifelong passion for reading became ours as well.

Though some people may have seen Mrs. Smallwood as old-fashioned, her exuberant approach to life and learning created a legacy for her students that can only be described as timeless.

Mike Brush

when learning
is fun

RELEARNING FRENCH

Some of the best learning happens when you're grown and out of school—when you're learning by choice. Twenty years after taking French, I could barely remember *bonjour*. So before going to France, my husband and I signed up with a private tutor.

We asked Kate to teach us French, but she teaches us much more—about travel, culture, history and, most important, about *joie de vivre.* Kate takes such delight in every day. We exchange books and videos, and we chat about everything from cooking to our cats—*en français,* of course.

When learning is that much fun, you learn more. On our last trip to France, a hotel manager said that I spoke French well.

Merci, Kate!

Alarie Tennille

SOMETHING REALLY SPECIAL

She was an outsider with fiery, shoulder-length hair that was on the last leg of its perm. She drove a once-red, rusted-out Volkswagen bug with balding tires and a dented bumper covered in antiwar stickers. She wore beaded necklaces, baggy clothes, and well-worn hippie clogs.

In those first few weeks, our seventh-grade class joked about all these things (and a few more) behind her back, but secretly, we all knew Ms. Wagner was something really special.

And for all her peculiarities to 32 inner-city kids, this tireless woman found so many ways, day after day, to open wide the windows of the world, just for us.

Who expected great things from each and every one of us and made learning challenging and fun?

Ms. Wagner.

Who stayed on even after she caught the entire class cheating on her very first English test?

Ms. Wagner.

Who had really nice penmanship, played a mean tambourine during choir, and even invited us to her very own wedding?

Ms. Wagner.

Who came in early and stayed late because she chose to and gently extracted "can't" from our collective vocabulary?

Ms. Wagner.

Who touched more lives than she may ever know?

Ms. Wagner.

Tom Shay-Zapien

A LOVING SPIRIT

Mrs. Hyde was a hugger. You know the type. The teacher whose arms were always wide open in welcome, making all the little someones in her class feel loved and cherished. Those hugs really made a difference my third-grade year. Shy and worrying about my parents' divorce, I came to school many days uncertain of myself and the world around me. But Mrs. Hyde was right there with a warm smile, an encouraging word, and an extra hug or two. Recognizing how much I loved to read, she even appointed me class librarian. She always seemed to know just the thing a child needed.

Years later, while home from college, I stopped by Mrs. Hyde's house one afternoon. She told me about retired life, and I told her about my literature courses. She was so pleased to know I still loved to read. Before I left, she placed a small jar in my hand labeled "hugs." "For when you need an extra one or two," she said.

To this day, years after that afternoon and her later passing, I think of Mrs. Hyde and her loving spirit every time I see that jar sitting in its special place on my bookshelf. She was a teacher whose first priority was taking care of little hearts. From the bottom of mine, I will always be grateful.

Suzanne Berry

Taking care of little hearts

The Compassionate Woman

IMAGINE WHAT IT WOULD BE LIKE

We moved to a new neighborhood when my daughter Kathleen was in fifth grade. From her very first day at school, her classmates teased her for being overweight. After two weeks of this cruel treatment, Kathleen refused to return to school. Her insightful teacher, Mrs. Harrison, took action.

"This morning, I want you to imagine what it would be like to be Kathleen," she said, her voice kind but firm. "What if you were different? How would it feel to eat lunch alone every day?"

The students squirmed at first, then opened up and began brainstorming ways to stop the bullying and welcome my daughter into their world.

Kathleen eventually returned to school. And to her amazement, the teasing had stopped. By initiating a simple dialogue with her students, this compassionate woman awakened her students to the importance of empathy and understanding.

By refusing to accept meanness in her classroom, Mrs. Harrison turned Kathleen's life around.

Molly Wigand

A TASTE OF SUCCESS

For me, high school was a time of trying to balance being too cool to care and really caring a lot. Wanting to stand out while still fitting in, I still hadn't found the courage to really stretch myself instead of just getting by, when Mrs. Wilcox showed me that success has its own sweet rewards.

She was a new teacher but not a young one. With several teenagers of her own, she had already learned a thing or two about motivating kids. In her classes, there weren't any discipline problems because her approach was to focus so much on success that there wasn't time for acting up. She believed in positive reinforcement and threw out candy for correct answers on verbal quizzes. For outstanding work on an assignment or top scores on a test, she gave out ice cream gift certificates. We were supposed to be too mature and cool for such "childish" things, but her excitement for learning and success was contagious. She always expected us to try, and so we did. In her own way, she made it fun to be a little better than ordinary and helped us taste the sweetness of success.

Beverly Laudie

No one
INFLUENCES
the future more
than parents
and teachers.

MATHEMAGICAL

After every test in my senior-year trigonometry class, I remember thinking, That's it. I have reached my mathematical limit. I can do no more. But the very next day, I'd find myself pushing a little farther, "getting" a little bit more, all because of the excellence of my teacher.

Mathematical thinking was clearly a talent for Miss Edwards. Cosines and tangents were her friends. She could work a problem like magic, but she didn't assume that everyone else could. She was the absolute best at breaking a solution down into simple steps until—eureka!—I had the magic, too.

One day when I was particularly mystified, I remember Miss Edwards telling me, "You can do this." And to my complete amazement, after a few minutes of her one-on-one help, I could.

I got A's in the class both semesters, but I'm sorry to say that the magic has since left me. I'd be stumped if presented with a trig problem today. But I know Miss Edwards stretched my brain in lasting ways, and the most enduring mind-opener of all was this: not everything will come easily, but with a little help and a little effort, you can always do more than you thought you could.

Keely Chace

A GIFT OF MUSIC

As a young boy, I found piano lessons tedious and boring, so after a few years, my parents let me quit. But then I found that it wasn't playing the piano I hated, but the lessons. So Dad introduced me to a friend of his who taught piano, Mrs. Mitzimberg. She made piano fun! Sure, I had to do the drills, but she gave me appealing music to learn. She also taught me how to play by ear, a skill I put to good use much later by playing honky-tonk and ragtime in a restaurant to help keep the wolves from the door when my family was young.

My daughter Melissa, now grown, recently told me that she used to love it when I played "The Entertainer" in the family room at night as she was about to go to bed. She would listen at the heat grate in her room, and now, every time she hears that song, she recalls the tond memory of her dad playing the piano.

So wherever you are, Mrs. Mitzimberg, thanks for the gift of music.

Richard Bagley

Bringing ideas to life

HELP AT EVERY TURN

Sometimes teachers sacrifice for us in ways we don't fully appreciate until much later.

Miss Lane was my high school English teacher and drama coach. My two passions at the time were writing and acting, so I naturally took many of her classes and performed in plays she directed.

Our drama program included an event where senior drama students directed one-act plays. I ambitiously decided to write my own play and apply to produce it. Without thinking much about the demands it placed on my teacher, I included a part for a pianist who would play a very difficult Beethoven sonata.

Not only was Miss Lane receptive to the idea, but she helped me at every turn. She offered suggestions for improving the script and guided my first tentative steps into the world of directing. Somehow, she even found money in the drama budget to hire a prominent local musician to play the role of the pianist.

It was only years later that I realized how much extra work Miss Lane had done to help bring my idea to life. To this day, I'm grateful to her.

Scott Emmons

SKULLCRACKER

That was our nickname for one of the fifth-grade teachers at our school. We quaked in fear as fifth grade approached, having heard "Skullcracker" stories from the older kids. Which of us would be placed in her class? Which of us would survive?

Many "Skullcracker" stories were apocryphal. That didn't put a dent in the fear we all felt, though. Whether "Skullcracker" really hung students by their thumbs in the coat room till they starved or whether that was just a rumor, it worked.

Yet every Friday afternoon, "Skullcracker" would read to us out of a mystery book, acting out all the parts, assuming different voices for the different characters. All we

had to do was listen—and enjoy! She called this "reading for pleasure" and made sure we liked the idea. Like Sheherezade, she would always end the reading hour just as something hair-raising happened in the book!

It's those reading hours I remember today... not the supposedly mean things. Her "meanness" was probably a somewhat cultivated and wildly exaggerated reputation. I just know I picked up a lifelong interest in reading for pleasure in "Skullcracker's" classroom.

Ellen Brenneman

MR. BILL'S BLISS

Mr. Bill, my freshman year high school drama teacher, is still the coolest guy I've ever known. His ineffable grace and subtlety made even his criticism poetry. He taught theatre not because he was a failed actor, but because it was his bliss.

Every drama class with Mr. Bill was an experience of incredible growth. He'd sit on the edge of the stage glowing with energy as he'd offer constructive insight–never lecturing, always discussing as if we were working actors. And it made us believe in ourselves.

As freshman year ended, Mr. Bill, setting aside a major precedent, handpicked me to join the upperclassmen's Theatre Arts Workshop for the next year. Previously, you couldn't get in unless you were a junior and had passed the audition. I was ecstatic and amazed, but Mr. Bill saw something in me I hadn't seen in myself. It gave me strength.

That summer, I took history while Mr. Bill team taught summer theatre. A week into the summer term, I walked into class to find my history teacher, pale and shaking, announce, "Mr. Bill just had a heart attack and died on stage in the arms of his students." As devastated as I was and as much as I still miss him, I remember "in the arms of his students" and smile. He followed his dreams, and what happened? Bliss.

Linda Morris

THE EVERYDAY THINGS

Dr. Koivisto was the home economics teacher at my junior high school. At a time when many teachers were sitting on the edge of their desks, shooting the breeze with the kids, Dr. Koivisto was stern, exacting, and strict. It was clear that she saw her job as teacher more than friend.

The desk-sitting teachers were my favorites at the time, but it's Dr. Koivisto's lessons that have stayed with me all these years.

I have forgotten how to diagram a sentence. But I can quickly rattle off the four components of a successful sandwich.

I can't recite the binomial theorem, but I know how to sew on a button so it will never come off.

The events that triggered World War I have slipped my mind, but it's okay, because I know how to use a pumice stone.

I know how to tell if a bra fits properly and that if I stir the batter too much, I'll get tunnels in the muffins. I can straighten the grain of a piece of fabric, and I know that three teaspoons equal a tablespoon.

So thanks, Dr. Koivisto, for these practical lessons. I think of you every day when I use the everyday things you taught with so much care.

Molly Wigand

Lessons that stayed with me

THANKS FOR CARING

My daughter attended a typical suburban elementary school, but there was nothing typical about the teachers who worked there. Every morning, she walked into an aisle of hugs as teachers hugged each child walking by on their way to class. Can you imagine what a great start to each day that is?

My daughter took a tumble on the playground one day when she was in the third grade. She twisted her ankle badly and was taken to the nurse's office. I was called to come pick her up and get the ankle x-rayed. Hearing of the mishap, the teacher she'd had in first grade gave up her break to comfort and soothe my daughter until I arrived. I found a calm third grader thanks to the consideration and sacrifice of that teacher.

The students at that school received a wonderful education, and they were surrounded by a staff of concerned teachers who cared about the whole student... not just the scores on the aptitude tests. Our family will always remember the difference those dedicated teachers made in my daughter's life.

Debbie Lorenzi

Behind every
SUCCESSFUL
person there is
a dedicated teacher.

A GIFT FROM THE PASTE BOY

For Miss Emerson's birthday, I wanted a gift that would show how much I loved her. And why not? Because of her, I loved first grade.

I'd just moved from a tiny rural school, and Miss Emerson saw how agonizingly withdrawn I was. She understood the timid lives little kids lead and how important belonging is. So she sat me beside the most talkative girl in class. And she gave me a job—paste boy. I'd go around importantly with a jar and scoop out paste for everyone. When kids ate the paste, I'd rat them out. Miss Emerson gave them a disappointed look, and no one wanted that. Always speaking in a mild, kindly voice, she was loved by all.

On the night before I needed the gift, I told Mom. She didn't drive, and Dad was on the road selling to drugstores. Improvising, Mom picked a wholesale unit of roll-on deodorant from Dad's drugstore samples and wrapped it up with a bow.

Opening my gift, Miss Emerson grinned like I'd given her the Hope Diamond. She told me in secret it was her best gift ever. (Other kids gave gifts, too—I didn't care what she whispered to them.) I just knew that I would do or learn anything to make Miss Emerson happy.

John Peterson

TRULY COOL

Mrs. Theiss was no match for a classroom of too-cool-for-school sophomores. She'd start a typical English class by talking about proper essay-writing techniques. We'd roll our eyes and say, "But Mrs. Theiss, what about...?"

Our "what about" questions could be anything from the fight that broke out after the homecoming game to a recent news story about whether or not it was right to force kids to recite the Pledge of Allegiance in schools. She always took the bait, and we reveled in our ability to get her off-track.

"Prove it!" she'd say whenever we took an unqualified stand on anything. "Explain yourself!" she'd admonish in response to vague platitudes. By the end of the class, we'd be so far afield from essay writing, we wondered how she managed to keep her job.

"Write up your ideas," she'd call out to us as we left the room. "We'll talk more about this in our next class."

Pretty smart, eh? We sure thought so. It took me quite a few years to realize how Mrs. Theiss had managed to outsmart us! By corralling our passions, she had helped us to become critical thinkers and effective communicators. Way to go, Mrs. Theiss. Now I know it was you who was truly cool.

Lisa Riggin

BOLSTERING A GUY'S CONFIDENCE

The transition from junior high to high school is traumatic for most kids, particularly if you're like me: skinny, pimply-faced, not a whole lot on the ball, and afraid of my own shadow. I could have become one of the Lost Souls of high school—you know the ones—with the forlorn yearbook pictures, weird hair, and nothing noted next to their names.

One teacher, Miss Herrick, made all the difference for me. Miss Herrick taught drama. She looked like somebody's great-aunt—short, plump, gray hair. She got me involved in drama. I wasn't an actor (that became immediately obvious), but she helped me find my niche in the technical side of things—sound, lights, sets. The cavernous school auditorium became my sanctuary. I nearly lived there, working under the stage, above the stage, behind the stage—anywhere but on the stage. I became indispensable. Miss Herrick once said she wanted to marry me. (This was before there were rules against teachers saying that sort of thing.)

Just knowing there are women who want to marry you has a way of bolstering a guy's self-confidence. I got involved in choir, band, and the school paper. I even managed to get a date to a dance or two. In the end, my yearbook picture had a respectable number of notations. I still had weird hair, though.

Tracy Icenogle

She made
all the
difference

He made me feel better

A LESSON ON PERSPECTIVE

I was doing a sad sophomore slouch down the high school hallway when Mr. Schelling came up beside me. He was the football coach; I only knew him because we went to the same church.

"Who are you going to winter formal with, Sarah?" he said, making small talk. The lockers were plastered with posters advertising the annual ball.

I looked down. "I don't have a date."

"Does that bother you?"

"Um. A little." A lot, I thought. A date was social currency. Approval. Assurance that you were okay. Normal. Liked.

He smiled sympathetically, and we turned down opposite halls.

A few days later, I got a letter from Mr. Schelling. In it, he related my winter formal woes with those of a former star player who was at college now and also having trouble finding dates. Mr. Schelling said we were both victims of a strange social phenomenon wherein smart, capable, attractive people aren't asked out because they are too intimidating. He said not to worry; life is more than your sophomore winter formal.

Whether or not this was entirely true (I had a feeling my shyness and flat chest were also to blame), it made me feel better. With one first-class stamp, Mr. Schelling lifted me out of the vortex of teen angst and taught me a lesson on perspective I've never forgotten.

Sarah Mueller

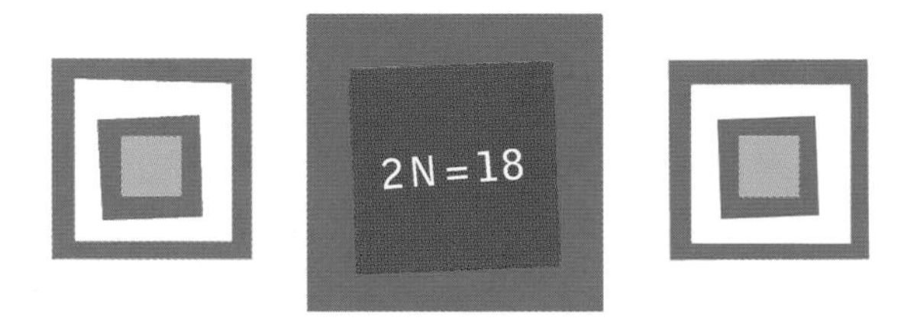

SARGE

Miss McCarthy was my algebra teacher. We called her Sarge because the former nun ran her classroom like boot camp. When the bell rang, the drill began—Sarge, sitting front and center at an overhead projector, would introduce the skill, then break it down through an hour's worth of examples, while we copied everything she did. It was relentless, no-nonsense, and effective... just like Sarge. In her class, you acquired superior math skills and learned to keep "your mind on your business and your business on your mind."

But one day, she taught us something else. It was one of those late-year, sunny afternoons, when being stuck in a classroom was torture, yet Sarge was mercilessly grinding through a tedious lesson. Suddenly, the longest, loudest tire screech I'd ever heard interrupted class. We waited in silence for a thundering crash, but...nothing. That's when Dave, notorious smart aleck and bane of Sarge's existence, calmly announced, "Mom's here."

We fell out of our chairs. So did Sarge. Watching her stoic face melt into wild laughter was like witnessing history. That day, we loved her even more for showing us two things—that it's okay to laugh now and then and that she was human, too. Thanks, Sarge. I've forgotten most of the algebra, but I'll never forget you.

Sarah Summers

A PERSONAL GIFT

My family valued education and reading, but they had no interest in art. Neither did our public schools. So, when Mrs. Moran, my American History teacher, announced she was launching a pilot course in Humanities my senior year, I felt she was giving me a personal gift.

I never enjoyed history classes, with their emphasis on politics, wars, and dates. I wanted to know how people lived, what music they heard, and what their houses, clothes, and paintings looked like. Mrs. Moran's Humanities class filled in those pieces.

She took us to museums, played music in class, and even invited us to her home, filled with antiques and fine art. When she served me orange spiced tea in delicate

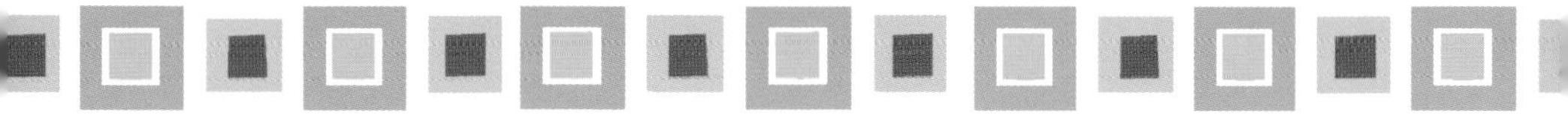

Japanese tea cups, I wanted to be adopted!

We lived close to Colonial Williamsburg, so I had been there many times before. But Mrs. Moran took us on a scavenger hunt: we each had to locate a mansard roof, dentil moldings, Chippendale railings, and other architectural features on the buildings. Williamsburg became mine that day. I'll always remember that, and it led me to sign up for more architectural history in college.

Mrs. Moran brought history to life.

Alarie Tennille

LEARNING TO LOVE WORDS

Ms. Nagel was a legend at my high school. She was a big, brassy, smart-as-a-whip, serious-as-a-heart-attack English teacher. Her desk was a mess and so was her hair, as if lashed by the hurricane force of her personality. She was fierce in her love of literature and told us to "read everything, especially books that seem dangerous."

I wrote my first serious poem in Ms. Nagel's class. Oh, I'd written doggerel and limericks and generic haiku. But Ms. Nagel put your poem up on the wall, via overhead projector, and you read it aloud, and then the class discussed it, just as we discussed famous "real" poems. It made you look at your words in a whole new light, literally. You took poetry to heart in that class, as if it could change the world—or at least change your heart. It made me want to be a poet.

And I became one. That first poem, which I cringe to think of today, led to many others. I won poetry prizes in college, got published in small journals, wooed my wife with poems, and landed a job because I could write them. I'm still writing them. And for me and every other student who learned from Ms. Nagel to love words, the legend lives on.

Jim Howard

As they pass
through our lives,
we call them teachers,
but in our hearts,
we call them
HEROES.

SHOES TO FILL

She was petite—no taller than most of the fifth graders in our class. What I noticed right away was her small feet—no bigger, I judged, than my 11-year-old feet. The possibility of playing dress-up in high heels just my size captured my imagination. So I asked Mrs. Johnson if she would give me a pair of her worn-out high-heeled shoes. Was she astonished at this brazen request? I can only imagine! I'm sure she was reluctant, because I remember reminding her many times of my request. What a pest!

That year, Mrs. Johnson taught me American geography (my state was Wisconsin) and dragged me through long division. I read the whole series of Black Stallion books and began to write poems. But high heels were always on my mind. On the last day of the school year, she produced the shoes, a pair of strappy white high heels I'll never forget. I nearly broke my ankle learning to walk in them that summer.

Mrs. Johnson, you were the kindest teacher ever, and no one, not even I, could ever fill your shoes.

Barbara Loots

GOOD MEMORIES

Walking into Miss Sibyl's piano studio was like walking into a dollhouse parlor. A black upright sat in the room amongst tiny antiques, fragrant candles, and little bowls of colorful candies. In the midst of it all, was I—never on rhythm and always using the wrong fingers; every piano teacher's nemesis, no doubt. But Miss Sibyl didn't seem to mind. She sat by my side, surviving my stop-and-start clunking, managing to smile. She knew how to bring out my strengths, like my memory skills. Every time I memorized a section, she'd place a shiny, gold star on my music. When I played the entire piece by heart, I'd get three stars. I memorized one book after another because she was there, each week, teaching me the importance of practice, dedication, and accomplishment.

Recently, I went back to visit Miss Sibyl. She had moved into a bigger studio, but it was still as charming as ever. Seeing her after so many years, I couldn't help but get a lump in my throat as I was transported back to that star-dusted time of my childhood. We talked about the things that had changed. Sadly, her husband had passed away. Her grandchildren had grown up, too. When I told her I majored in music, she told me she was so proud.

I still have a good memory, Miss Sibyl. And I remember you.

Katherine Stano

A SIDEWALK MOMENT

It would be an understatement to say our daughter has always been strong-willed. Yes, she could be cajoled and convinced on occasion, but there were plenty of times when even large amounts of patience didn't work.

Mrs. Beatty, her second-grade teacher, found this out shortly after the school year began when Bess simply vanished from class early one morning.

A vague response from a classmate prompted Mrs. Beatty to look out the window. Sure enough, Bess was purposefully walking away from the school, nearing the corner.

She had escaped the watchful eyes of teachers and administrative personnel, breezed through the school's main entrance, and as we would soon learn that afternoon, was determined to walk home after suffering an injustice that was never fully explained.

Fortunately, Mrs. Beatty quickly and calmly resolved the episode by arranging to leave the building, catching up to Bess, gaining her trust, soothing her wounded sensibilities, and gently guiding her back to the classroom—all within a few minutes.

Perhaps more importantly is what Mrs. Beatty didn't do. She didn't panic, alert anxious students and punitive administrators, or treat Bess like a seven-year-old fugitive. It was a small personal matter that simply required a quiet moment of understanding.

In that moment on the sidewalk, student and teacher became friends through second grade and still today, almost twenty years later.

Ed Wallerstein

DEAR DR. BRADLEY

Seventh grade is not an easy time for blossoming adolescents, and I was certainly no exception. With my mouth full of braces and newly permed poodle hair—life was tough.

Your class was one of the best things about that year for me. Every single day, you were so full of energy! You led animated discussions about famous quotes and literature. You encouraged the whole class to speak our minds and express ourselves through writing—sometimes getting so excited about something we wrote that you'd actually jump up on your desk. You once did that for a poem I wrote, and thinking back to that still makes me smile.

You were fun. You made me want to learn. But most of all, you helped me to feel good about myself. At least during your class, I would forget about the braces and bad hair.

Today my braces are long gone and my hair has grown out, but my memories of you still remain.

Melissa Woo

WINDOWS TO THE WORLD

Huge windows lined one wall of our seemingly ancient ninth-grade English classroom. Through them, we could look down on the park nearby and the bustling streets of our little downtown. That was "the world" to me then—the one I'd daydream about as I gazed out those windows.

But inside that classroom was where everything was really coming alive, as our teacher, Mr. Peterson, opened the window of literature for me. I felt like I was really seeing and understanding the world for the first time. We read *To Kill a Mockingbird* and had great class discussions about "walking in another person's shoes." We wrote little plays in small groups and performed them for the class. We listened to the lyrics of current Simon and Garfunkel songs and analyzed them as poetry. Up to that time, I had struggled in school, but in Mr. Peterson's class, I was finally finding success and discovering my passion for the written word. Mr Peterson knew how to engage his students and show them the world through the window glass of literature.

As winter gave way to spring, the world outside those classroom windows was changing before our eyes. And as I watched the new buds unfolding on the branches, I remember feeling that I, too, was unfolding—becoming something new, someone fully alive, thanks to Mr. Peterson.

Diana Manning

Teachers take us to faraway lands, places we might have never known without them. They give us tools to succeed that otherwise we might have

never found, and they make
us feel better about ourselves
than we might have if they
hadn't believed in us.

If you have enjoyed this book,
Hallmark would love
to hear from you.

PLEASE SEND COMMENTS TO

Book Feedback
2501 McGee, Mail Drop 215
Kansas City, MO 64141-6580

OR E-MAIL US AT:

booknotes@hallmark.com